INVESTING: A BEGINNER'S GUIDE FOR LONG TERM SUCCESS

Stanley H. Bryce

INTRODUCTION

GENERAL

Investing can be defined as the act of spending money or capital on endeavors with the expectation of receiving additional income or profit. Essentially, it is a completely different way to think about the way money is made. Growing up, many of us learnt that we can only earn income by working and this is exactly what many people are doing right now. However, there is one big issue and that is if you want more money, you're probably going to have to work for more hours. This probably won't make that much money for you and will exhaust you both mentally and physically. Also, you can't possibly create another version of yourself to increase the time you spend time working. Investing your money isn't going to maximize the potential of your earning whether you choose or not to work overtime, get a bonus, or look for another job.

There are various ways you can choose to make any investment. This involves placing money into stocks, mutual funds, real estate, and even investing in other businesses. Experts refer to these choices as investment vehicles, which each one having its own benefits and drawbacks. However, it is essential that you choose an investment vehicle after you have spent enough time looking through the different options and understanding them. You should also avoid following others 'investment strategies because success in the investing world differs from one person to another. For example, someone might be more comfortable investing in three investment vehicles because they have been in the field for years whereas this isn't recommended for someone who is just starting out because they are most likely going to get confused. It is always better to succeed in one and then jump to the next one.

One important thing you need to understand is that investment is completely different from gambling. Gambling involves you placing money at risk by bettering on unknown results with the hope that you will win money. At gambling the odds are always against you however in investment you can shift the odds to your advantage. However, some of the confusion between investing and gambling can come from the way people use investment vehicles. For example, purchasing a stock because someone told you is just like placing bets in casinos. However, real investors don't simply throw their money at any investment out there; they perform analysis and spend capital and money only where reasonable profits are expected. Even though there is a risk, there aren't any guarantees whatsoever and investing is more than just hoping that you get lucky.

This book includes a detailed explanation on investing, its various associated terminologies, methods of investing, among other important information that will get you started in the world of investing.

CHAPTER 1 - BASICS ON INVESTING

EXPLORING POSSIBILITIES OF INVESTING

The world of investing is diverse and full of different possibilities and chances. One of the best things about the investment world is that there is a place for everyone. Whether you're a beginner or have been investing for years, have long or short-term goals, or simply just want to experiment a bit, you will definitely find something suitable for you. However, it is essential to understand that this isn't a get rich quick scheme where you're going to make millions overnight. You will first need to educate yourself about its different aspects, set your goals, and choose what you want to invest in. Becoming successful in the investment world requires hard work, dedication, and a proper understanding of its different aspects. This chapter is going to involve a detailed explanation of the different types of investment vehicles, their benefits and drawbacks, and the steps required to successfully invest in them.

STOCKS & BONDS

Stocks and bonds are two important investing building blocks. Stocks are direct ownerships in businesses whereas bonds are loans. Various products related to stock and bonds have been created during the past few years, such as mutual funds and default swaps. These investment choices are great, but with these choices is the responsibility to recognize which of these choices help you in fulfilling financial goals. Buying stock means that you're going to take ownership in a specific entity. One of the main advantages of direct ownership is that the process is fairly easily and there aren't any associated management fees or other individuals involved. The price of buying individual stocks is affordable – many times, it can cost $10 or even less. However, one of the drawbacks is that you have to stay updated on how the investments are doing all the time. This is why you need to at least have a proper understanding of accounting principles and stay updated with company reports. Buying bonds means that you're going to loan money to entities, like businesses, people, or governments. Purchasing a bond is exactly like purchasing a car: you need to negotiate so you can get the better price. Owning a bond needs you to know the claims you have to the entity's assets if bankruptcy takes place.

Changes in the market can have a big impact on stock markets as well.

The Dow jones is considered to be one of the biggest financial markets. Every day, traders engage in $5 trillion worth of exchange transactions. Due to Dow Jones being an international marketplace, events taking place from all over the world can have an instant impact on currency values and rates of exchange. This report is going to explain the impact of global events on the Dow Jones market (Jones &

Khanna, 2006). During the year 2015, there were several events that affected Dow Jones such as the Greek crisis, the decrease of oil prices, and the change that took place in the Federal Reserve interest rate policies,

Greek crisis and its impact on Dow Jones

When the Greek crisis took place, Dow Jones decreased to the lowest rates and it was considered to be the worst day for it in 2015. The significant decline was a result of Greece closing their banking system, central bank executing controls to stop money from leaving Greece, and all the different protests that took place as a result where citizens weren't happy with all the changes that were taking place (Consolandi, 2009).

Traders stated that the selling process was mainly broad based. Volumes of trading were somewhat high, with 7.3 billion shares continuously changing hands when compared with the annual data average of about 6 billion shares. The Dow industrials decreased by 350.33 points, to 17596.35. On the other hand, the S&P 500 decreased by 43.85 points to 2057.64. Finally, the Nasdaq index decreased by 122.04 to 4958.47.

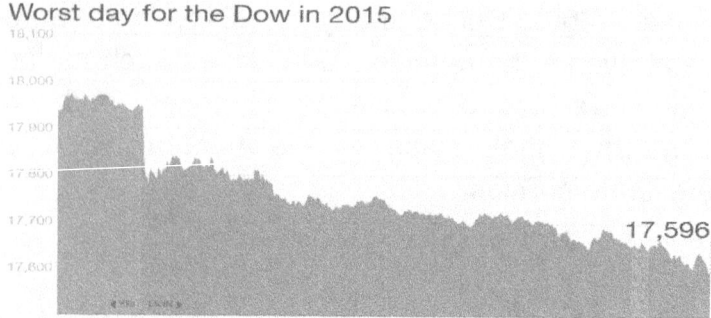

Worst day for the Dow in 2015

17,596

9:30AM 11AM 12PM 1PM 2PM 3PM

Figure 1: Dow Jones decline due to the Greek crisis

Source: CNN money

Decrease of oil prices

In August, oil prices decreased below $40 per barrel and this is the first time this happens since 2009 amongst increased agreement that cheap crude is going to stay. Oil investors, who figured it out early that prices are going to recover during the second half of this year, now state that rebounds are most likely going to happen before 2017. Government forecasters decreased their estimates of oil prices to $60 per barrel during 2016.

The change in opinions is mainly because of oil producers in the United States, who are continuously pumping crude at record levels. An unexpected rally of prices that took place in some companies enabled companies to lock profitable prices for 2016. Brent crude, the international benchmark decreased by 2.5% to about $45.46 per barrel.

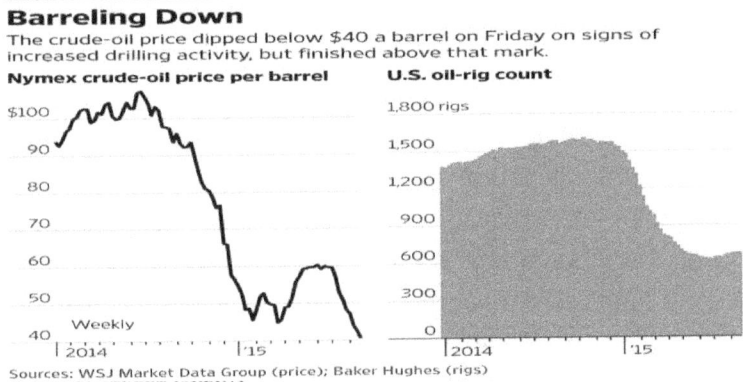

Barreling Down
The crude-oil price dipped below $40 a barrel on Friday on signs of increased drilling activity, but finished above that mark.

Nymex crude-oil price per barrel   U.S. oil-rig count

Sources: WSJ Market Data Group (price); Baker Hughes (rigs)
THE WALL STREET JOURNAL.

Figure 2: Impact of market changes on stock prices

Source: WSG

Federal Reserve interest rate policies

During the end of 2015, the Federal Reserve decided to increase interest rates, and this had a significant impact on the stock market, especially Dow Jones. This is the first time this happens in nine years and no one excepted this surge to take place. This had a positive impact on stocks, where the Down Jones increased by 185 points, Nasdaq increased by 1.1%, and the S&P 500 increased by 1.3%. It was a unanimous decision to increase rates and Fed officially asserted that even though the rates increase, the policy will still be accommodative. The Federal Reserve policy has helped in increasing stocks in the United States since the crisis took place. The dollar decreased against the euro. Also, the yen government bonds became stronger, pushing yields to an even lower rate. Stocks that pay out dividends high in value, which has continuously rallied in previous years among low rates of interest, resulted in the S$P 500 become higher after the decision of the Feds. The prices of crude oil increased to 4.9 per barrel, snapping rebounds for two days, after an increase in the crude supplies in the United States. This surge took place suddenly and wasn't expected at all. On the other hand, stock markets in other regions such as Europe and Asia weren't open in trading when the Federal Reserve released their new decision. This is one of the very few events that had a positive impact on Dow Jones and associated trading processes during 2015.

During the year 2015, there were several events that affected Dow Jones such as the Greek crisis, the decrease of oil prices, and the change that took place in the Federal Reserve interest rate policies. This report included an explanation of the different events that impact Dow Jones. These situations include wars, natural disasters, and political events. Each of these events has both a negative and positive impact and it can be difficult to determine what exactly is going to take place and whether traders are going to gain or lose money. Even though traders can predict certain events before they take place, it is difficult to do this in every situation, especially like the case of natural disasters where no one actually knows when they're going to take place. Also, it is difficult to predict how an event is going to impact Dow Jones. As demonstrated in this research, there are some cases where wars in example impacted S & P positively and some cases where it affected it negatively.

MUTUAL FUNDS

Mutual funds are a method for investors to place their money in one place, so they can increase purchasing power and decrease execution costs. One of the drawbacks to mutual funds is the different associated fees. All types of mutual funds charge a fee, and many even charge sales fees on top of management fees. If you choose to invest in mutual funds, make sure you completely understand the fees you have to pay and the investment fund mandates. It is essential to note that you will only be able to trade mutual funds once per day and that is when the markets close.

EXCHANGE TRADED FUND

The Exchange Traded Fund (ETF) is a financial innovation that is newer than the other investment vehicles. The ETF places mutual funds into an investment vehicle that trades likes stocks and works due to the one price law. The one price law explains that when two investments track the exact same thing, then the profit and return from holding these investments is going to be the same as well. For example, when investments are overvalued, you are going to sell these overvalued investments and then use the returns to purchase more of the accurately priced investments. However, if you decide to buy an ETF, make sure you pay attention to what the investments being tracked are, and the amount of ETF shares being purchased and sold on a daily basis.

It is essential to check on who is responsible for sponsoring ETF functions and make sure that it is done properly. All these different investment vehicles are excellent investment tools and every one of them has a place in a well-diversified plan.

REAL ESTATE

Investing in real estate has become more popular during the last fifty years and is considered to be one of the most important investment vehicles. Even though the real estate market has numerous opportunities for making money, purchasing, and owning real estate, this is more complicated than simply investing in stocks or bonds.

Basic rental properties

This is one of the oldest real estate investment practices. It involves someone purchasing property and then renting it to tenants. Owners are responsible for paying mortgages and costs associated with maintaining the property. Landlords can charge extra to cover aforementioned costs and to produce a profit for themselves. Furthermore, the property can be appreciated in terms of value.

A main difference between rental properties and other investment types is the time and work spent on maintaining the investment. When you purchase a stock, it's going to stay in your investing accounting and increase in value.

Real estate investment groups

Real estate investment groups are similar to mutual funds for rental properties and are the perfect choice for you if you aren't looking for the hassle of taking responsibility as landlords. An example of this would be purchasing apartment blocks and then enabling investors to purchase them through the company, therefore joining investment groups. Single investors are able to own numerous or one complex. In exchange for this type of management, the company is going to be able to take a part of the monthly rent. Even though this is definitely safe way to enter the real estate investment sector, many groups are susceptible to the exact fees that trouble the mutual fund sector.

REAL ESTATE TRADING

This is considered to be real estate's wild side. Real estate traders purchase properties with the purpose of holding them for a specific amount of time, often not more than four months, hoping to sell them in return for a profit. This technique is known as flipping properties as well and depends on purchasing properties that are undervalued or in hot markets. Pure property filters aren't just going to put money in real estate for enhancement's where the investment needs to have intrinsic values, so it can gain profit without any alteration or they won't even take it into consideration. Flipping in this way is considered to be a short-term investment. If property fillers become caught in situations where they can't unload properties, this can be overwhelming, as these investors don't maintain enough cash, so they can pay mortgages on long term properties. This can result in continued losses for real estate traders who are not able to offload real estate in poor performing markets.

REITs

An interesting fact is that real estate has been in the world since our ancestors, so it isn't surprising that Wall Street was successful in finding a way to transform real estate into an instrument that is publicly traded. Real estate investment trusts (REIT) is created when an organization (or the trust) utilizes the money of investors to operate and buy income properties. REITs are purchased and sold on major types of exchanges, like other types of stocks. Companies have to pay 90% of their taxable profits in the type of dividends, to maintain its position as an REIT.

RUNNING SMALL BUSINESS AND INVESTING IN THEM

Investing in other start-ups

Investing in established businesses or start-ups can be a successful investment and more profitable than you expect. Venture capital funds that are publicly traded usually invest in different start-ups, resulting in then creating a diverse portfolio of companies that have the potential to be successful. With only one investment, you are going to be able to access a diverse portfolio of companies that have successfully passed venture capital tests. There are usually many chances to make direct investments in start-ups that you have some knowledge or experience in, where you can exchange equity stakes for the funding you provide.

Both investment types have a level of outsized risks that matches outsized rewards if the business proves to be successful. Therefore, it is essential to do research and invest in these opportunities. Investing your money through venture capital is the most popular alternative. You don't necessarily have to leave your job or establish an office; you will only have to purchase shares.

Partner Up

Instead of only investing in businesses for equity stakes, you should consider taking it into another level and become a partner in a business that already exists. This is going to include making daily work in the organization, focusing on things founders don't necessarily have enough time for, such as market or accounting, or it can possibly be a larger role. Not only is it going to provide you with the entrepreneurship experience, but enable you to select the types of tasks and work you would like to do.

INTRAPRENEURSHIP

Another choice is becoming an intrapreneurship in larger companies. Many organizations have established structures that persuade employees to lead new organizational lines in exchange for equity and bonuses. When you find an organization that has a powerful innovation culture, you are going to be able to build your own organization within it, with the benefit of having start-up capital from the start and personal risk is going to decrease as well.

You could even be able to begin an interpretership program at your work by asking for an amount of your time to work on projects that have bonus structures. To boost your argument, you can always boost to companies such as 3M and Intel, two companies which experienced significant growth throughout a period when interpretership defined corporate culture.

PURCHASE A FRANCHISE

Businesses in boxes are one way to steer away from the hassles involved with beginning from scratch. Owners of franchises already follow scripts that have already proven to be successful. The advantages of franchises include dealing with a well-known brand, having resources to go back to, and economies of scale created by franchises.

The main disadvantage is the cost of purchasing a franchise and its associated royalties, which are really steep most of the time. Individuals looking for the true entrepreneur experience are going to have issues with various limitations added by franchise offices. However, franchises usually have a powerful support network and are known for having high rates of success.

CHAPTER 2 - RISK AND RETURN

Understanding the concept of risk, returns, diversification, and portfolio building is extremely important in the investment world. This chapter includes a detailed explanation of these aspects along with steps on how to successfully build a diversification portfolio.

RISK AND RETURNS IN THE INVESTMENT WORLD

There are risks that investors face in the investment world. Many of these risks are serious, and if not addressed properly, can have negative long-term impacts on the ability to fulfill your financial goals, and others are simply considered to be driven by feelings and human bias. A type of risk includes the organization you're investing in going bankrupt, which means that you're going to lose money. However, this doesn't necessarily happen a lot and the results can be decreased by diversification and not following the promise of high returns.

Diversification is an effective way to manage risk. Usually, investment advisers and managers speak about risks like interest rate, market, and currency risks. Every one of them can result in returns and profits being less than what is expected and, in many times, even negative. However, they are all considered to be manageable and are essential parts of the more significant risks.

This usually takes place when investors are too conservative, inexperienced, greedy, or simply give up a lot of their returns for taxes or fees. In many cases, there are going to be event risks that are going to have an unpredicted negative effect on your assets values. As example of this would be foot disease in New Zealand.

However, the good news is that there are principles you can follow to successfully manage risk such as:

- There are no returns without associated risks. The returns are only half of the equation. Earnings that are higher than long-term profits usually have more short-term risks. The profits and rewards are reaped by investors who manage these risks and don't search to prevent risk altogether. Risk is considered to be the other side of the chance of the investment. What is essential is that risks you take are appropriate for the investment you're making and the time frame of your financial goals.
- Risks should be properly understood and returns have to be completely transparent. When risks associated with investments aren't understood properly, it is going to be difficult to manage them. If returns 'sources aren't transparent, associated risks are a lot higher as of the unknown. Investing first needs information and understanding and using common sense.

- Experience and count of judgement. Risks can't be controlled only using mathematical models or ratios. A risk reward tool is used by many investors to conduct a comparison of an investment's expected returns to the risk amount undertaken to get these returns. They are simply a tool that creates the basis of the right judgment.
- Diversification. This is going to be explained in more detail in the next part. Diversification includes various investments, in one asset class, decreases risk without changing expected returns. Diversification also decreases uncertainty level that the outcome of returns is usually different.
- Consistency. A rigorous and steady approach will lead in managing risk better than a process that is constantly changing. It also offers an improved framework for comprehending the outcome. It is also essential to comprehend where competitive advantages can be found and the decisions that can be made based on this guess.

CONCEPT OF PORTFOLIO BUILDING AND DIVERSIFICATION

There are some situations where checking the value of your investments can be tempting. However, this is just when feelings have a strange way of stopping the minds of even the most experienced investors. This is the main reason why you have to check your portfolio on a regular basis, at least the investment mix once per day or any time you notice your financial condition changing significantly. For example, when you lose your job or receive a significant bonus. Setting your strategic asset share are among the most significant ingredient in your long-term success.

WHY DIVERSIFY

The main goal of diversification isn't only to enhance performance as it won't guarantee profits or losses. However, once you select to focus on a risk level depending on your objectives time horizon, and acceptance for volatility, diversification can offer the chance to enhance returns for that risk level. To successfully create a diversified portfolio, you need to search for assets and investment vehicles, whose returns didn't move in the exact same direction. This way, when a part of your portfolio isn't performing well, the remaining part of your portfolio will be growing. Therefore, you will be able to offset the effect on poor performance and prevent it from negatively impacting your portfolio. Another essential aspect of creating a well-diversified portfolio is that you can attempt to stay diversified within every investment type. With the holdings of your individual stocks, make sure you avoid single stock overconcentration. For example, there is the possibility that you don't want a stock to be worth more than 5% of your overall stock portfolio.

Diversification has proven to be successful

Throughout the 2008 bear market, various investment types have lost their value to an extent. Even though it seemed like diversification failed, it actually didn't. The significant asset classes were actually more correlated, and diversification still assisted buy-and-hold portfolio losses. Take into considered 3 hypothetical portfolios: a portfolio including 70% stocks, 25% short term investments and finally 25% bonds.

Diversification assisted reduce losses and maintain gains throughout the financial crisis

	Jan. 2008 through the market bottom, Feb. 2009.	Five years from the bottom: Mar. 2009–Feb. 2014	2008 to five years from bottom: Jan. 2008–Feb. 2014
All-cash portfolio	1.6%	0.3%	2.0%
Diversified portfolio	−35.0%	99.7%	29.9%
All-stock portfolio	−49.7%	162.3%	31.8%

Source: Strategic Advisers, Inc.

The asset's hypothetical value maintained untaxed accounts worth $100,000 in cash portfolios. This is a diversified portfolio including 49% local U.S. stocks, and 21% global stocks. By the end of February 2009, both stocks and diversified portfolio declined. However, they all lost half of their initial value. On the other hand, the diversified portfolio lost more than a third. Even though the diversified portfolio could have decreased, diversification would have assisted in decreasing losses when compared with all-stock portfolios.

Investors have lower returns than some of the indexes in the market

January 2004,- December 2014

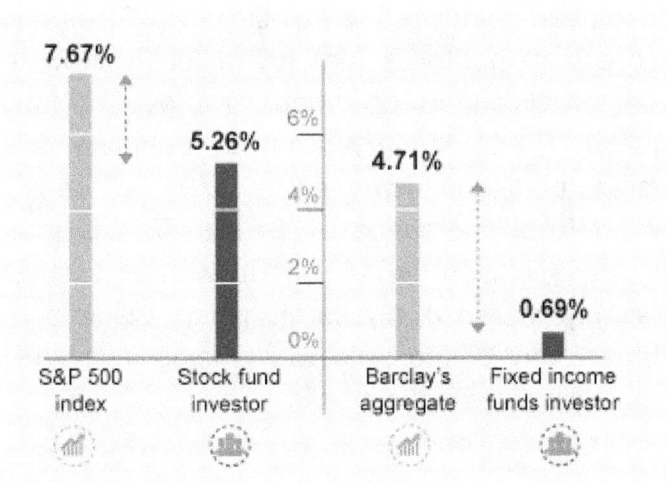

Source: Quantitative Analysis of Investor Behavior (QAIB) 2015

Watching stocks and diversified portfolio decrease if the type of situation that can stress investors or stir their emotions. This can sometimes result in making short-term and fast decisions, such as dumping stock holdings. Yes, keeping money in the form of cash could have sounded like a great idea during February 2009. However, look at what ended up happening when the market began becoming stable again.

5 years after being in the bottom, our created all-stock portfolio would have increased by 162.3% and the diversification portfolio would have been worth around 99.7% more. All stock portfolios experience the biggest improvement during the upswing of the markets. This is an excellent example of the way portfolios can gain less than all-stock portfolios and a lot more than portfolios that are all-cash. Now let's look at what ended up happening over a longer sequence. From January 2008 to February 2014, diversified portfolios increased by 29.9% whereas all-stock portfolios increased by 31.8%. This is mainly what diversification is all about where it doesn't necessarily increase profits in rising markets, but captures many of the gain while being less volatile than investing in various stocks

THE HIGH COST OF CHOOSING BAD TIMING

Why is it essential to have a level of risk you can live with? As the above chart demonstrates, diversified portfolios end up playing over time. However, the fact is that many investors face issues to realize the advantages of their investment tactics, individuals usually go after performance and buy higher-risk investments.

When the market faces issues, investors usually go for lower risk investment choices. These choices can result in missed chances during consequent market recoveries. The extent of underperformance by these investors has proven to be the worst in bear markets. Research have consistently demonstrated that returns gained by average stocks and bonds, fund investors lag usually by large margins, reported returns and profits of average stocks.

Research conducted from DALBAR demonstrates that fund investors follow markets in a significant manner. This means that most of the decisions they make related to diversification generate lower returns than overall markets. Having a well thought plan that consists of suitable investment mixes and proper rebalancing can assist investors in overcoming these issues successfully.

How to Build a Diversified Portfolio

To begin, you are going to have to make sure that your investment vehicles and mix are aligned with your investment duration, financial requirements, and comfort with levels of volatility. Previous performance isn't a guarantee of how your investment vehicles will act or future results. Returns consist of reinvesting dividends and other types of earnings. However, it is essential to understand that diversification isn't a one-time task and investments usually change over time. The chart below demonstrates the difference between the performance of diversification portfolios in 1995 and 2015.

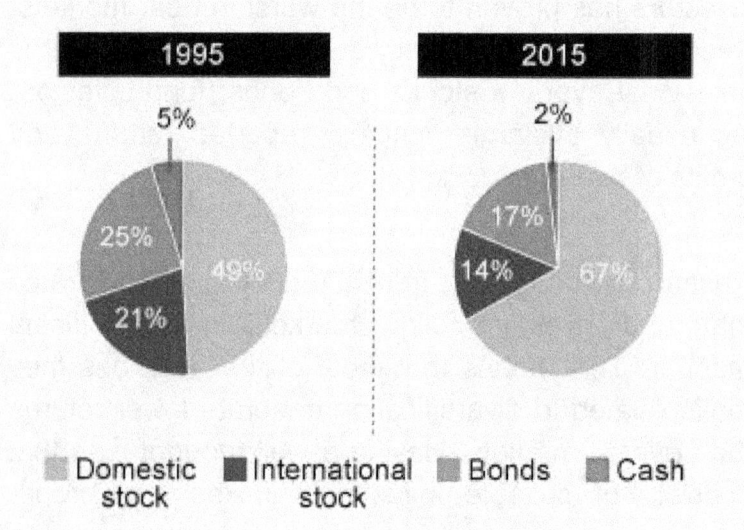

Data Source: Ibbotson Associates, 2015 (1926–2014).

This chart's illustration is only hypothetical and uses monthly performance from 1995 until 2015. Stocks are demonstrated by S&P 500 whereas bonds are demonstrated using Barclays intermediate Treasury bond indexes. Finally, short term investments are demonstrated using the U.S. thirty-day T-bills. When you have a target mix, it is essential that you maintain it and ensure its on track using periodic checkups and reevaluations. When you don't reevaluate your portfolio, this can leave your portfolio with high level of risk that is unsuitable with your overall goal and plan.

So, what actually takes place when you don't balance your portfolio? Let's examine an example portfolio over a twenty-year period to show how changing markets, like the S&P 500's increase which took place in last years, can have an effect on investment mixes and risk levels in portfolios. Let's say the portfolio experienced a growth worth 80% in stocks, 10% in bonds, and 10% in short term investments during April 1995. Twenty years later, at the end of April 2015, this mix has completely changed, and all its components experienced an increase.

An important thing to understand is that previous performance doesn't necessarily guarantee profitable results, especially that stocks have had higher cost swings than money or bonds. In other words, when portfolios tilt towards stocks, they have the chance for bigger increases. The risk level of the portfolio was about 10% more than target mixes because of changes in the allocation of assets related with relative returns to the different investment vehicles. The levels of risk associated with the portfolio are assessed by the yearly standard deviation of returns gained every month, which demonstrated the variability of returns.

Let's now examine these levels of risk over time by taking two scenarios as an example. If investment mixes are rebalanced back to targets on a yearly basis, and if no revaluations took place (a purchase and hold technique). The levels of risk associated with purchase and hold portfolios differs widely than the ones of rebalanced portfolios. Throughout the time frame, this portfolio will have higher risks (yearly portfolio volatility). Rebalancing and reassessing your portfolio aren't only an exercise to decrease risk. The main goal here is to rearrange your investment mix so it is brought back to the expected levels of risk. Sometimes, this can mean decreasing risk levels by increasing portfolio portions in more conservative choices. However, this can mean increasing the risk, so you can get back to the target mix again. This involves increasing the amount of investments in asset classes that are more risky like stocks. You will have to create a strategy, select suitable investment, and carry out regular checkups to make sure that your portfolio is always on track. Below are three steps that are going to help you in achieving this:

I)KNOW WHAT YOU INVESTMENT MIX IS.

(April 1995-March 2015)

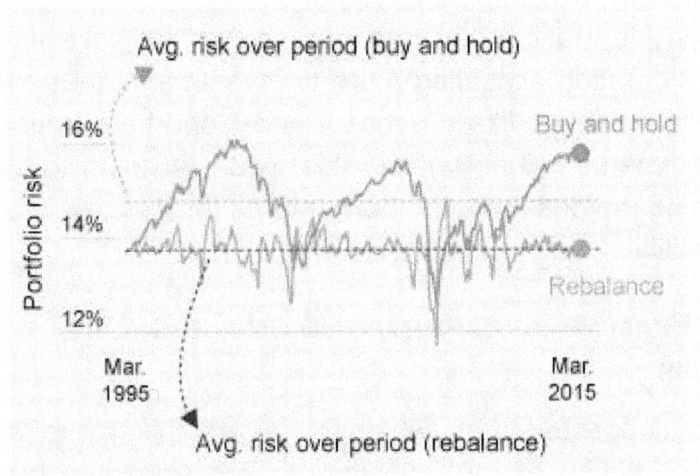

Source: Quantitative Analysis of Investor Behavior (QAIB) 2015

The chart above is for demonstrative reasons only. It shows observed historical risk associated with performance of diversified indexes. Portfolios that aren't diversified in any asset classes can go through various levels of risk.

If you haven't done this already, select a combination of investment vehicles that you consider suitable for your investing objectives and goals. You should also take into consideration your finance, levels of volatility, and you will require the money you're investing. The more time you have to investment, the higher the appropriate level of investment vehicles in a portfolio. For example, stocks have always higher growth possibilities, and longer time frames can assist in decreasing volatility levels. Also, when you require the money in a couple of years, or if the idea of losing money is making you nervous, you should take into consideration allocating more to investments that are less volatile like bonds and short duration investments. When you do this, you are going to be trading the possibility of more returns for less levels of volatility.

II) EXAMINE YOUR PORTFOLIO ON A REGULAR BASIS

It is suggested that, whether you do this alone or using the help of investment professionals, you should monitor investment mixes on a yearly basis, or whenever the market conditions or financial circumstances end up changing. It is essential that you reassess your portfolio to fix any significant change that is going to impact your portfolio. A good idea is to considered rebalancing your portfolio is the stock allocation shifts away from the target by 10% points

III) REBALANCING YOUR PORTFOLIO

There are different ways to rebalance your investment portfolio. One of them is to sell these assets classes that you have a lot of and then reinvest these gains in those that are less than your target. However, selling securities in accounts that are taxable has different tax consequences. Therefore, you have to be sure to take taxes into consideration when you're making a decision to purchase or sell. Another way to do this is by rebalancing the portfolio without instant tax results in by investing the money have gradually or at the same time.

No matter what approach you decide to follow, one significant part of rebalancing is to do it in a manner that keeps your investing portfolio diversified in any investment type. Fulfilling your long-term goals needs balancing rewards and associated risks. Select the right investment mixes and then monitoring these choices can make a huge difference in your results.

CHAPTER 3 - GETTING STARTED

After choosing an investment vehicle and the type of portfolio you're interested in, the next step would be selecting an appropriate strategy. This chapter is going to include a detailed explanation of the investment process, how to successfully set up goals, and effective ways to create a portfolio.

FOLLOW THE INVESTMENT PROCESS

The investment process is divided into seven different steps, with each one being more important than the other.

- Purpose: You need to ensure that you have a proper understanding on the aim of your investments, in relation with your goals and the reasons you're investing your money in them. You should have different short-term goals in the framework on a long-term plan. However, various investments are more suitable to various goals and this is why you have to take into consideration every goal separately and differently, and then search for synergies between these goals.
- Return: Choose the returns you need, in terms of immediate or long-term income. This also includes growth and development to successfully achieve goals. Income and components of growth are going to make up for the total profits and returns.

- Time frame: Choose the time frame you're investing for, so you can achieve and make progress when it comes to achieving your objectives and goals. Your time frame is going to be a mixture of the timeframe you want to spend your money on (example: retirement) and the maximum amount of time you can wait before you see profits and any results. This is going to make you confident that you're on the right way to achieve your objectives and goals.
- Risk: choose which risks and the amount of risks you're going to take. You should also choose risks and possible adverse results that can and have to be managed.
- Investment tactic: choose the investment strategy that is best for you in terms of balancing the requirements of your returns over the duration you're investing in.
- Assets: choose the type of assets (products) you are going to purchase to apply your plan.
- Review: Make sure you repeat these stages, as needed, based on any changes that take place to your objectives or any sudden circumstances that take place.

When you follow the seven-step investment strategy, you will find that you need assistance and recommendations if you're just starting out. If you don't need help, then that is great, and you can continue implementing the steps on your own. If you do, it is a great idea to discuss your objectives and goals with someone who is more professional and will help you in being objective. Likewise, when you identify assets for your investment strategy, you could need someone with a specific expertise. However, it is essential to remember that the more fees you pay to gain advice and help, the less returns you are probably going to end up with. The recommendations obtained should focus on enhancing the chance that you can fulfill your financial goals.

CREATE AN OVERVIEW OF YOU FINANCIALS AND DECIDE HOW MUCH YOU ARE WILLING TO USE FOR INVESTMENT AND THE IMPORTANCE OF MAINTAINING LIQUIDITY.

Creating an overview of the amount of money you're going to spend and understanding the concept of liquidity is important. Do you understand how money that is easily accessible is in the shape of cash and equivalent's? This is a liquidity assessment.

As you can see, this has a significant role in the financial lives and those of the stocks you purchase and sell. Beginning from a definition of it with examples of various types, we then going to examine how investment vehicles have an essential role in maintaining liquidity. It is essential to understand liquidity from the point of view of other investors, especially when it comes to the stock market. Keep in mind that financial ratios could be used to assess the liquidity of an investment vehicle or a company.

Liquidity refers to how easy it is to transform assets to money (cash). Cash is considered to be the most liquid assets, and this is why it is always used for comparisons. On the other hand, deposit certificates are considered to be less liquid, as there is a penalty for changing them to cash right before their date of maturity. Also, savings bonds are considered to be quite liquid, because they're sold at banks in an easy manner. Finally, the different shares of bonds, commodities, and stocks are considered to be somewhat liquid, as they are sold readily, and cash can be received in a couple of days. Any of these can be considered to be cash or equivalents of cash as they are converted to cash without any effort, even though this can sometimes be accompanied with a small penalty.

Moving down, we are going to run into different assets that require more effort and time before they could be considered to be cash. An example of this would be restricted shares, which has covenants dictating the way it can possibly be sold. Other examples include items such as coins, arts, and other types of collectibles. If you are going to sell other collectors, you should receive full value, but this can actually take some time, even with the internet making it easier to some extent. If you take the decision to use a dealer, you are going to be able to receive quicker, but it is probably going to be less. The least type of liquid asset is real estate as it usually takes weeks, if not months to be successfully sold. When investing in assets, it is essential to take levels of liquidity in considered as it can be hard, or it can take a lot of time to chance certain types of assets into cash again.

Apart from selling assets, cash could be gained by borrowing against it. Even though this can be done in a private manner between two individuals, it is usually done thought financial institutions. A financial institution has a lot more cash from depositors put together and can effectively fulfil the requirements of any borrower. Also, when depositors require cash instantly, this person isn't just going to withdraw it from the financial institution instead of going to borrowers and asking for payments of the whole note. Therefore, financial institutions act as intermediaries between the lenders and borrowers, resulting in a smooth money flow and fulfilling the requirements of every part of a loan.

LIQUIDITY AND STOCK MARKETS

When it comes to the stock market, liquidity has a different meaning, even though still connected how easily the assets, or stock shares, can be effectively changed to cash. The stock market is considered to be liquid if shares are rapidly sold and selling acts have little effect on the price of stocks. Usually, this translates to where shares are bought and traded and the amount of interest that the investors have in it. The stocks of companies traded on significant exchanges are considered to be liquid. Usually, 1% of the overall float trades on a daily basis, showing high interest degrees in stocks. Also, stocks of companies traded on pink sheets and over the counter are considered to be non-liquid, with a few, if not zero shares traded on a daily basis.

Another way to successfully judge company's stock liquidity is by examining bid/ask spread. When it comes to liquid spreads, like Microsoft and General Electric, spreads are considered to be a couple of pennies only, probably less than one percent of the overall price. However, when it comes to illiquid stocks, the spreads are considered to be a lot larger, resulting in a few percent of the overall price.

An important thing to take into consideration as an investor when putting an order, is the stock's liquidity. During ordinary market hours on significant exchanges, putting a limit order will lead to you getting the price of what you're looking for. This is especially true for non-liquid companies, or throughout after hours trading where fewer traders are going to be active. It is the most suitable to put a limited order as lower liquidities can result to a cost they wouldn't be willing to pay.

DEFINE FINANCIAL GOALS AND CREATE OVERVIEW OF EXPENSES (FINANCIAL TRIANGLE → LIQUIDITY, RETURN, SECURITY (MONEY).

The next and perhaps one of the most important steps is clearly defining short term and long-term goals. It is essential to also understand and follow the financial triangle, which includes liquidity, return, and security where they are all connected to each other.

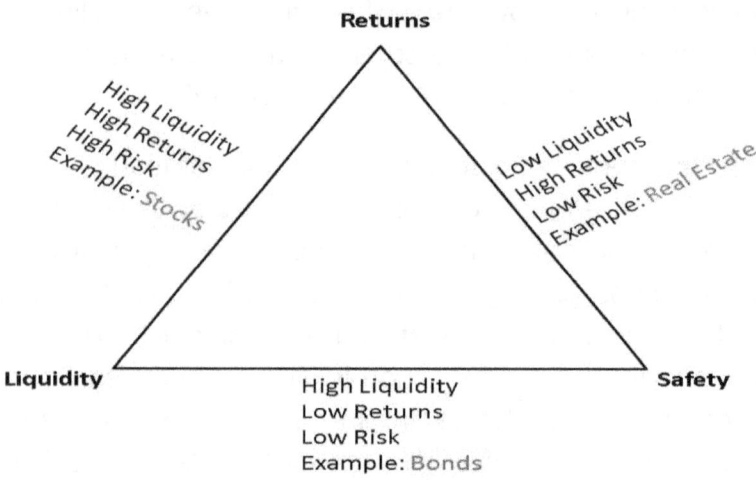

Source: Strategic Advisers, Inc.

People invest for different reasons and this is why it is important that you determine your financial goals, both long and short term. You could have to spend years on some goals whereas other can be achievable within a couple of days. Relatedly, it requires careful planning and a more balanced approach to successfully fulfill long term goals while financing current ones.

When you're creating the financial strategy, the main thing you have to do is figure out your short- and long-term goals. This will provide you with assurance of a promising financial future. With goals and an investment plan being clearly identified, there will be a tendency to place your money in the wrong place with useless spending resulting in the possibility of financial trouble. Think of the goals you set as the framework for your investment plan. Every financial goal needs to have a time frame and is considered to be a milestone for future goals. Short term goals are different from long ones in timing. They are usually smaller in their scope and monetary amount with a specific target date for achieving them.

Example of short-term goals could involve buying household furniture, home improvements, or simply saving to invest in a stock. A short-term goal is one that you could possibly want to achieve a couple of weeks to two years from the time you invest. Many investment experts explain that short term goals should involve eliminating any debt and having an overview of expenses.

IDENTIFY AND PRIORITIZE GOALS

The first thing you have to do is figure out the things you want in life. This could differ from purchasing a house to beginning a business or simply retiring based on your schedule. Without any goals, the returns you earn can be spent on things you don't necessarily require at that moment of time. Other than identifying financial goals, try to estimate the amount of expenses and money you are going to require so you can reach every goal. Creating a time frame for every short-term goal is important as well, especially when it comes to determining how many years it is going to take you to successfully achieve this goal.

Assessing finances and eliminating debt

Examine your current financial situation, such as credit card debt, loans, or mortgages. Before you begin investing money and spending money to achieve goals, it is essential that you eliminate any debt you have, especially ones that have high interest rates such as credit cards. This actually has to be your main short-term goal. Also, if you have purchased stocks and funds previously and these investments are doing well, make sure they fit into your plan. Understand what exactly you're basing the goals on. For example, if you're setting goals for retirement, you need to figure out the amount of years left until you retire, and the income amount you are going to need. The next short-term goal is enhancing savings by reducing on unwarranted spending. When you take a look at some of things you spend money on, you will notice that there are a lot of things you spend on that aren't necessary and you can use them in the investment process.

Asking for help in setting up a financial plan is a great idea as well if you're facing issues understanding certain aspects. Investment advisors who are experienced aren't only going to assist in identifying goals and evaluating a financial situation, but they are also going to choose investments that are matched with your objectives and goals. Also, investment advisors are specially trained, so they can find investments that are suitable with your strategy, risk place, and also taking into consideration different aspects of your life into consideration when creating an investment plan for you. Expert investment advisors also conduct regular follow-ups by continuously monitoring investments and ensure adjustments are made when required.

LONG-TERM GOALS

There are short term, long term, and goals that are simply in between. The difference between these categories is usually connected to the time it requires to fulfill the goals and the monetary commitment to fulfill them. Long term goals usually require years to be calculated. The most essential long-term goal for everybody is saving for their retirement or making enough money so they can support the lifestyle they want on a long-term scale. One of the main steps involves excellent savings and creating a detailed financial plan when you are starting out. This will enable you to stay on track throughout the process.

MONITOR INVESTMENTS ON A REGULAR BASIS

It is essential to check investment on a regular basis. It is recommended to personally go through your portfolio every four months and meet with your advisor on a regular basis. You should also manage risks by ensuring your selected assets allocations are still matching with your overall objectives and goals. Make suitable adjustments to investments only when required. The main benefit of having investment advisors is that they're going to be able to monitor funds and encourage various investments when needed. If something comes up when you're reviewing your plan, you can always revise it accordingly because this is going to help you in identifying new goals as well.

DEFINE A PORTFOLIO OF YOUR INVESTING STRATEGY (EG.. 20% STOCKS, 50% COMMODITIES, 30% REAL ESTATE)

In today international marketplace, an investment portfolio that is well-maintained is essential to the success of any investors. As an investor, you have to know the way to figure out an asset that is suitable to your investment goals. Also, your portfolio has to fulfill your future needs and provide you with comfort and peace of mind. It is essential that portfolios are aligned with goals and investment plans by following a detailed approach. Here are some steps you should follow when you're defining and creating your investment portfolio:

1. Determining the suitable asset allocation: determining your financial situations and goals is the first step in building a portfolio. Essential

items to take into consideration are age, the amount of time you need to develop these investments, and the amount of capital needed to invest along with future needs. For example, a single graduate student just starting his career and a 70-year-old person who is married and wants to retire soon are going to have various investment plans.

2. Achieving the planned portfolio designed in the first step. When you have determined the correct asset allocation, you have to divide this capital among suitable asset classes. This isn't going to be difficult on a basic level where equities are going to be equities and bonds will definitely be bonds. However, you can later on divide various asset classes into smaller categories or subclasses, which can have various risks and possible returns. Many investors choose to separate equity portions among various sectors, domestic, and international stocks. The portion of bonds could be allocated among them can be short or long term.

3. Re-evaluating portfolio weightings: when you have created a portfolio, you have to assess and rebalance it in a periodic manner due to market movements, which can cause initial weightings to transform. To assess your portfolio's actual asset allocation, quantitatively categorize the investments and determine their values' proportion to the whole. Other factors

that can change by time are the financial situation, potential needs, and tolerance for associated risks. When these things change, you are going to have to change or regulate your portfolio based on them. When the risk tolerance decreases, you are going to have to decrease the quantity of equities held. Also, you are going to have be ready to accept a greater risk and the allocation of your asset needs a smaller proportion of the assets to be placed in small caps stocks that are somewhat riskier.

4. Rebalancing the portfolio in a strategic manner. When you have determined the type of securities you want to decrease, and by which amount, you should make a decision of the underweighted securities you will purchase with these proceeds. This also involves selling securities that are overweight or aren't leading to as much profits as expected. To select your securities, you should go for the second step. When you sell the assets to reassess your portfolio, you should time to take into consider tax implications associated with reassessing the portfolio. Perhaps the investment process is growth stocks have continuously appreciated during the previous year. In this situation, it could be beneficial to not contribute new funds to the class further one because this is going to decreasing the weighting of the stocks in the portfolio by time with accumulating gains taxes.

THE FINAL LINE

Overall, a portfolio that is well-diversified is the best solution to ensure that your investments are continuously developing and growing on a long-term basis. This will also protect all your different assets from any risks of significant declines and different structural changes in the economy by time. Make sure that you regularly monitor the portfolio's diversification, make the necessary adjustments when it is needed, and you are going to enhance your opportunities of staying successful throughout their investment career.

CHAPTER 4 - PORTFOLIO BUILDING

After you have defined and created your investment portfolio, it is time for you to build on it and ensure that it is continuously successful. This chapter includes a detailed explanation of how to build on your portfolio, what a lazy portfolio is, and investing in different types of index ET along with its associated statistical advantages.

HOW TO BUILD A LAZY PORTFOLIO AND MAKE NICE PROFITS

Lazy portfolios are created to perform well in different market conditions. Most of them consist of a small amount of low-cost funds that can be easily being re-evaluated and re-balanced. The reason they are considered to be "lazy" is because investors can easily maintain the exact same asset allocation for extended time frames, because they general consist of thirty to forty percent bonds, and this percentage is suitable for many pre-retirement investors.

THREE FUND LAZY PORTFOLIOS

Three fund portfolios are one of the most important types of lazy portfolios and consist of three categories of bonds, total global market, and total American market. Also, you take in consideration that there are various close alternatives related to these funds, especially when buying them from Vanguards.

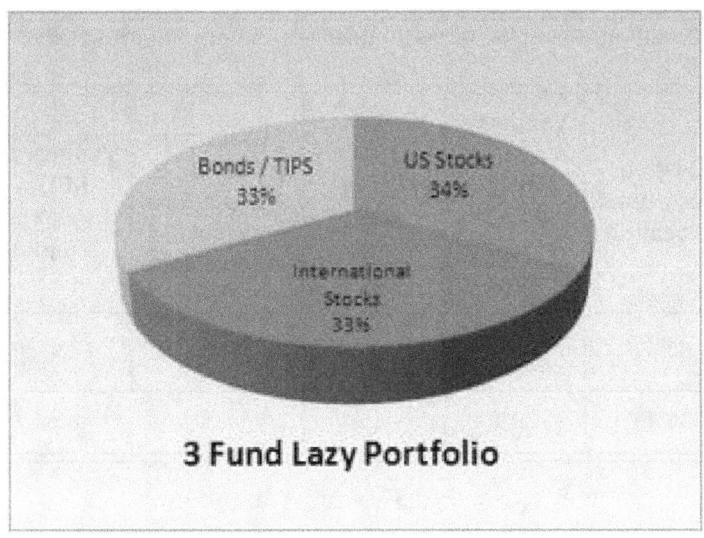

3 Fund Lazy Portfolio

Source: Bogleheads

CORE FOUR PORTFOLIOS

One of the simplest methods to create a portfolio is by core and extended holdings. The core holdings make up most of portfolio's associated risk and return features. Also, extended holdings provide the last touches to any portfolio. The core four portfolio includes four different types of funds which make up the portfolio's 'cornerstone'. The chart below demonstrates how assets are allocated in core four portfolios.

Core-Four Portfolio, Asset Allocations in Core Four Portfolio

Desired Stock/Bond Allocation	Vanguard Total Bond Market Index Fund	Vanguard Total Stock Market Index Fund	Vanguard Total International Stock Index Fund	Vanguard REIT Index Fund
60/40	40%	30%	24%	6%
80/20	20%	40%	32%	8%

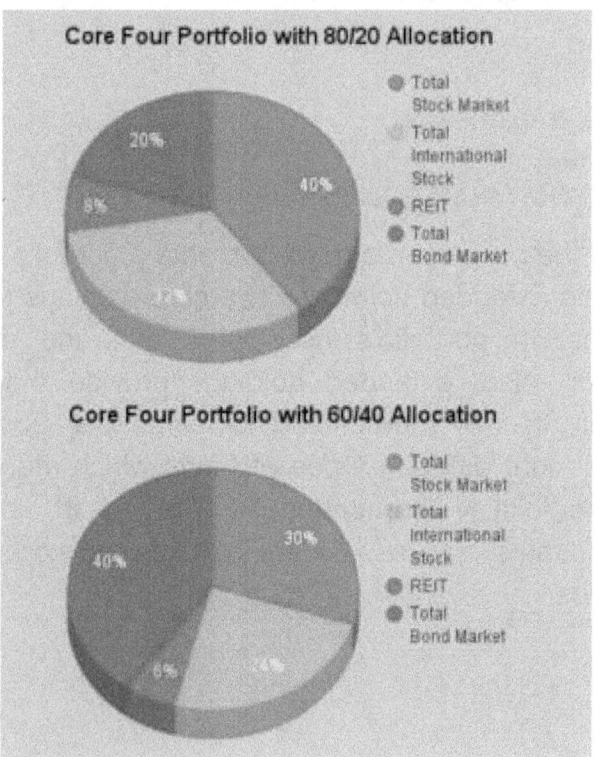

Source: Bogleheads

INVESTING IN INDEX ETFs WITH STATISTICAL ADVANTAGES

Investing in ETF is another excellent choice and there are many options to choose from.

- **Vanguard Total Stock Market ETF**: It includes 34% of the overall stock portfolio and follows the CRSP U.S. Total Stock Market index. It covers all the American stock market and has 19% of its overall assets in medium sized organizations and 9% in caps that are smaller. When compared, the S&P 500 has 12% placed in mid caps and there is nothing placed in small funds. Just like the case with all funds explained in this book, stocks are usually weighted using market value. This can be calculated by multiplying shares prices with the amount of shares outstanding. Apple currently has the largest holding with 2.3% of the overall assets. The value of the average market of the holdings related to funds is $37 billion. The funds currently yield 1.9% of expenses and 0.05% on a yearly basis.
- **Vanguard Total International Stock Index ETF**: this involves 22% of the overall stock portfolio and is the international twin of the Vanguard Total Stock Market ETF. It is reflected in the FTSE US Index where the average value of the market is about $21 billion. Markets that are somewhat developed

account for about 86% of the overall assets of the funds and emerging markets make up the rest. Bigger companies take over the funds, but about 17% of it is in mid caps and 3% is placed in smaller caps. The ETD currently yields about 2.8% and charges about 0.14% on a yearly basis.

- **Vanguard Dividend Appreciation Index ETF**: it includes 12% of the overall stock portfolio and involves only investing in companies that experienced an increase in its dividends during the last ten years. It follows the Nasdaq Dividend Achievers index, which eliminates companies that aren't financially strong, mainly because they have a lot of debt. Despite the focus of these dividends, it isn't really considered to be a high yield, just 2.0% which is like the S&P 500. Also, dividend appreciation is considered to be an unusual index fund, but the reason it was included was due to growing proof that high quality stocks, especially blue chips that have attractive dividends, have performed greatly on a long-term basis. Also, yearly expenses account for 0.10%.

- **Vanguard Extended Market Index ETF**: it includes 12% of the overall stock portfolio and follows the S&P Completion index. It almost owns every tradable American public company, not including penny stocks or anything similar, that the S&P 500 currently doesn't own. Ever since 1926, the small caps have gone through an average of 2% on a yearly basis higher than companies that are somewhat larger, even though with higher volatility levels. Almost 6% of the ETF is currently invested in mid caps along with small caps and charges 0.10% on a yearly basis.

- **Vanguard Emerging Markets Stock Index ETF**: it includes 8% of the overall stock portfolio, follows the FTSE Emerging Markets index, which consists of 850 stocks from twenty-two different developing countries. Markets that are emerging have followed US stocks ineffectively since the end of 2011. However, this doesn't necessarily mean that economies that grow quickly don't deserve to be included in your long-term investments. This fund currently charges 0.15% on a yearly basis. International stocks currently account thirty percent of assets, where 1/3 of them are emerging markets. During the last ten years in April 30, the investment portfolio returned a yearly 9.0%. By difference, the S&P 500 ended up returning a yearly 7.7% throughout the exact same stretch.

As far as investment vehicles are allocated, many investors should have about 70% to 75% of their investment portfolio placed in stock funds. However, it is recommended to gradually decrease that as you start approaching retirement. Even when retirement takes place, many individuals should try to keep 50% of their investments placed in stock funds.

CHAPTER 5 - SHUT DOWN THE MEDIA

DON'T BELIEVE EVERYTHING ON CNBC OR IN A STOCK MARKET MAGAZINE

One of the main mistakes that many investors do, especially beginners, is that they follow what investing magazines or channels tell them to do. Yes, they do give great advice and recommendations, but this doesn't necessarily mean they are going to work for you as well.

TIME BRINGS SUCCESS!

Educating yourself is very important and this has become easy with the endless sources available. Many successful investors were able to teach themselves by reading and studying these sources. There are books, articles, videos, and websites, paid and for free, which you can use to understand all the different aspects related to investing. There is nothing wrong with seeking help. If you feel that there is something you are unable to understand and need further assistance in, there is nothing wrong with contacting investment professionals who will assist you in anything you need.

No one becomes successful or rich overnight and this is one of the main misconceptions many investors have once they start investing. One of things you should never do is take this as a get rich quick scheme. Investing is something that takes time, dedication, and really hard work. Patience is really important as well. If you try a certain strategy for example, and it doesn't work out, keep on trying until you get it right. Everything is difficult in the beginning and investing is no exception to this rule.

CHAPTER 6 - RESOURCE'S

USEFUL WEBSITE LINKS FOR RESEARCH AND FURTHER CALCULATORS

COMPREHENSIVE

CBS MoneyWatch
http://www.cbsnews.com/moneywatch/

CBS Money watch provides the latest financial and stock market news. It also provides market quotes, financial advice, new related to markets, and a lot more.

CNN Money
http://money.cnn.com/

CNN money is a business site which provides the latest business, technology, markets, and personal finance news.

Investopedia
http://www.investopedia.com/

Investopedia is an all investment guide which includes theoretical and practical information that can be used to understand all the different aspects related to the investment world. This is an excellent choice for beginners who have no previous knowledge about investment strategies and its associated definitions.

Marketplace
http://www.marketplace.org/

Marketplace provides news related to financial companies and their performance on a daily basis. You will also find commentary and analysis conducted on the news reported.

StockTwits

http://stocktwits.com/

Stocktwits is more focused on the stock market and its different associated news and changes. It also includes stock market charts that investors can use to follow up on the performance of their stocks.

Yahoo! Finance

http://finance.yahoo.com/

Yahoo finance watch provides the latest financial and stock market news. It also provides market quotes, financial advice, new related to markets, and a lot more.

FINANCIAL NEWS/MARKET COMMENTARY

Bloomberg News
http://www.bloomberg.com/europe
Bloomberg news mainly focuses on financial related to Europe and UK, but you are also going to find international financial updates on a regular basis.

New York Times Business
nytimes

New York Times Business reports on financial and stock market related news in the USA but you are also going to find international financial updates on a regular basis.

Reuters
http://www.reuters.com/

Reuters provides constant and updated financial and business news from all over the world. They are considered to be among the fastest to report financial news and updates.

ECONOMICS AND BONDS

Calculated Risk
calculatedriskblog

Calculated risk enables investors to understand the amount of risk associated with investments they're interested in and understanding the overall concepts of risks and rewards.

The Dismal Scientist

dismal.com

Dismal Scientist reports financial news related to international economics on a daily basis. Financial data and analysis are provided by their expert economics team.

WSJ Real Time Economics

http://wsj.com/economics

The Wall Street Journal provides the latest financial and stock market news. It also provides market quotes, financial advice, new related to markets, and a lot more.

STOCK MARKET

SEC EDGAR

www.sec.gov/edgar/searchedgar/webusers.htm

SEC EDGAR collects documents to assist investors get data that is important for their investment decisions.

FreeStockCharts.com

www.freestockcharts.com

Free Stock Charts involve different charts that investors can use to monitor the performance of their investments and the stock market in general.

www.ingramcontent.com/pod-product-compliance
Lightning Source LLC
Chambersburg PA
CBHW070440180526
45158CB00019B/1800